Welcome to Dinks Dessert Shop!

We're delighted to welcome you to Dinks Dessert Shop, a beloved sweet spot in our charming Kentucky town. We're excited to share our most popular dessert recipes with you! Now you can easily create delightful treats that will impress your guests at potlucks, family gatherings, events, celebrations, farmers markets, and dessert bars at weddings and showers.

What makes our recipes special? They've been enjoyed by countless happy customers and are known for being reliable and crowd-pleasing. We're here to inspire you to bake, enjoy your time in the kitchen, and savor our amazing desserts at home!

Here at Dinks Dessert Shop, we love food and we love flavor. To create our unique recipes we use a blend of grocery store ingredients combined with exclusive commercial bakery grade products.

Please note that these recipes are the exclusive creations of Dinks Dessert Shop and may not be resold. If you have any questions or want to share your baking successes or happen to have any questions, we look forward to connecting with you on social media! Find us on Instagram and Facebook @DinksDessertShop.

TABLE OF CONTENTS:

COOKIES begin on page 4
- Bourbon Chocolate Pecan Cookie
- Chocolate Chip Cookie
- Cinnamon Chip Snickerdoodle Cookie
- No Bake Cookies
- Peanut Butter Cookie Sandwich w/PB Fluff
- Smores Marshmallow Stuffed Cookie
- Strawberry Cheesecake Cookie
- Sugar Cookie w/Royal Icing

CAKES begin on page 15
- Almond White Wedding Cake
- Cookie Butter Crunch Cake
- Carrot Cake
- Coffee Crumb Cake
- Cream Cheese Icing
- Hummingbird Cake
- Hybrid American Buttercream
- Italian Cream Cake
- Orange Juice Cake
- Red Velvet Cake
- Rum Cake
- Strawberry Crunch Cake

PIES begin on page 29
- Bourbon Chocolate Pecan Pie
- Buttermilk Chess Pie
- Chocolate Chess Pie
- Chocolate Cream Pie

- Coconut Cream Pie
- Pumpkin Pie
- Shortbread Pie Crust
- Stabilized Whipped Cream

BROWNIES & BARS begin on page 37
- Brown Butter White Chocolate Blondie
- Cookies & Cream Brownies
- Fudge Brownie w/Chocolate Buttercream
- Mississippi Mud Brownies
- Peanut Butter Buckeye Brownies
- Seven Layer Bars

NO-BAKE CHEESECAKES begin on page 47
- Plain Classic
- Cookies & Cream
- Dark Chocolate Raspberry
- Lemon
- Strawberry

ASSORTED OTHER DESSERTS begin on page 54
- Banana Pudding
- Banana Flip Twin Whoopie
- Peanut Butter Buckeyes
- Cannoli
- Cream Horn
- Tiramisu

BOURBON CHOCOLATE PECAN COOKIES

1.5 cups salted butter room temperature
1 cup white sugar
1 cup light brown sugar
1 cup dark brown sugar
2 eggs
4 Tablespoons bakers brand imitation vanilla
4 cups all purpose flour
1 small box instant vanilla pudding
3 Tablespoons cornstarch
7 ounces chopped pecan pieces
1 ounce Lorann brand oil bourbon flavoring
18 ounces mini semi sweet chocolate chips

Mix all of the wet ingredients with a mixer until well blended and fluffy and well combined, about 2 minutes. Add the dry ingredients to the wet. Blend ingredients by hand or mixer just until blended and all the white of the flower has been mixed in the wetness.

Now you want to refrigerate your dough in cling wrap/saran wrap for a minimum of 24 hours to a maximum of 72 hours. Do not skip this step. The ingredients get absorbed into each other and it makes for amazing science.

When you are ready to bake and allow your cookie dough to come to room temperature for about 1 hour. Preheat the oven to 415 and begin to scoop dough with an ice cream scoop sized to measure 2.0 ounces. Line your baking sheet with parchment paper and place 12 dough balls per sheet. This recipe will give you 35 sized 2 ounce scoops.

Bake for 11 minutes. Pull cookie sheet from the oven and allow cookies to come to a full cool at rest on the cookie sheet. Cookies will be fully set in 3-4 hours as the butter solidifies.

CHOCOLATE CHIP COOKIES

1.5 cups salted butter room temperature
1 cup white sugar
1 cup light brown sugar
1 cup dark brown sugar
2 eggs
4 Tablespoons bakers brand imitation vanilla
4 cups all purpose flour
3 ounces instant vanilla pudding
3 Tablespoons cornstarch
18 ounces mini semi sweet chocolate chips

Mix all of the wet ingredients with a mixer until well blended and fluffy and well combined, about 2 minutes. Add the dry ingredients to the wet. Blend ingredients by hand or mixer just until blended and all the white of the flower has been mixed in the wetness.

Now you want to refrigerate your dough in cling wrap/saran wrap for a minimum of 24 hours to a maximum of 72 hours. Do not skip this step. The ingredients get absorbed into each other and it makes for amazing science.

When you are ready to bake and allow your cookie dough to come to room temperature for about 1 hour. Preheat the oven to 415 and begin to scoop dough with an ice cream scoop sized to measure 2.0 ounces. Line your baking sheet with parchment paper and place 12 dough balls per sheet. This recipe will give you 35 sized 2 ounce scoops.

Bake for 11 minutes. Pull cookie sheet from the oven and allow cookies to come to a full cool at rest on the cookie sheet. Cookies will be fully set in 3-4 hours as the butter solidifies.

CINNAMON CHIP SNICKERDOODLE COOKIES

1.5 cups salted butter room temperature
1 cup white sugar
1 cup light brown sugar
1 cup dark brown sugar
2 eggs
4 Tablespoons bakers brand imitation vanilla

4 cups all purpose flour
3 ounces instant vanilla pudding
3 Tablespoons cornstarch
3 Tablespoons cinnamon
18 ounces cinnamon baking chips

Mix all of the wet ingredients with a mixer until well blended and fluffy and well combined, about 2 minutes. Add the dry ingredients to the wet. Blend ingredients by hand or mixer just until blended and all the white of the flower has been mixed in the wetness.

Now you want to refrigerate your dough in cling wrap/saran wrap for a minimum of 24 hours to a maximum of 72 hours. Do not skip this step. The ingredients get absorbed into each other and it makes for amazing science.

When you are ready to bake and allow your cookie dough to come to room temperature for about 1 hour. Preheat the oven to 415 and begin to scoop dough with an ice cream scoop sized to measure 2.0 ounces. Line your baking sheet with parchment paper and place 12 dough balls per sheet. This recipe will give you 35 sized 2 ounce scoops.

Bake for 11 minutes. Pull cookie sheet from the oven and allow cookies to come to a full cool at rest on the cookie sheet. Cookies will be fully set in 3-4 hours as the butter solidifies.

NO BAKE COOKIES

1/2 cup butter
1 3/4 cups granulated sugar
1/3 cup cocoa powder
1/2 cup milk
2 Tablespoons Lorann Butter Vanilla flavor emulsion
2/3 cup creamy peanut butter
3 cups quick cooking oats

Line two baking sheets with parchment paper or set out approximately 29 cupcake liners.
In a 3 quart medium saucepan combine butter, sugar, cocoa, and milk.

Set over medium heat, and cook stirring frequently until it reaches a full boil.

Allow the mixture to boil for 60 seconds without stirring.
Remove from heat, immediately add in vanilla, peanut butter and quick oats.

Stir mixture until well combined then using a cookie scoop drop mixture onto lined baking sheets or into cupcake liners.
Allow to rest until set about 30 minutes to speed up the set in the refrigerator.

PEANUT BUTTER SANDWICH WITH FLUFF

COOKIE DOUGH INGREDIENTS
3 sticks salted butter room temperature
1 cup white sugar
1 cup light brown sugar
1 cup dark brown sugar
2 eggs
4 Tablespoons bakers brand imitation vanilla
4 cups all purpose flour
1 small box instant vanilla pudding
3 Tablespoons cornstarch
20 ounces peanut butter chips
1 dram of Lorann brand oil peanut butter flavoring

PEANUT BUTTER FLUFF INGREDIENTS
16 ounces peanut butter
16 ounces wilton buttercream icing
6 ounces marshmallow fluff
1 Tablespoon heavy cream

Mix all of the wet ingredients with a mixer until well blended and fluffy and well combined, about 2 minutes. Add the dry ingredients to the wet. Blend ingredients by hand or mixer just until blended and all the white of the flower has been mixed in the wetness.

Now you want to refrigerate your dough in cling wrap/saran wrap for a minimum of 24 hours to a maximum of 72 hours. Do not skip this step. The ingredients get absorbed into each other and it makes for amazing science.

When you are ready to bake and allow your cookie dough to come to room temperature for about 1 hour. Preheat the oven to 415 and begin to scoop dough with an ice cream scoop sized to measure 2.0 ounces. Line your baking sheet with parchment paper and place 12 dough balls per sheet. This recipe will give you 35 sized 2 ounce scoops.

Bake for 11 minutes. Pull cookie sheet from the oven and allow cookies to come to a full cool at rest on the cookie sheet. Cookies will be fully set in 3-4 hours as the butter solidifies.

To make the fluff, mix all ingredients which will be very thick. Continue mixing until well combined. Use as a filling for sandwiches or dip.

SMORES STUFFED COOKIE

3 sticks salted butter room temperature
1 cup white sugar
1 cup light brown sugar

1 cup dark brown sugar
2 eggs
4 Tablespoons imitation vanilla
4 cups all purpose flour
1.5 ounces instant vanilla pudding
3 Tablespoons cornstarch
12 ounces semi sweet chocolate chunks
14 ounces graham crackers crushed
1 package 8.6 ounces Stuffed Puffs Filled Marshmallows (saved for Stuffing Stage)

Mix all of the wet ingredients with a mixer until well blended and fluffy and well combined, about 2 minutes. Add all dry ingredients to the wet mixture (except Stuffed Puffs). Blend ingredients by hand or mixer just until blended and all the white of the flower has been mixed in the wetness.

Now you are going to measure out 4-5 ounces of dough and roll it into a ball, making a hole in the middle enough room and now stuff the puffs inside. This will be approximately the size of a baseball. Now roll and seal your cookie ball, paying attention to make sure there are no openings in the ball. You are going to wrap your cookie balls in saran wrap. Now you want to refrigerate your dough in cling wrap/saran wrap for a minimum of 24 hours to a maximum of 72 hours.

When you are ready to bake, heat your oven to 415. Line your baking sheet with parchment paper and place 6 dough balls per sheet. This recipe gives you 12 large balls.

Bake for 16 minutes or just until the shine from the butter has disappeared. Pull cookie sheet from the oven and allow cookies to come to a full cool at rest on the cookie sheet. Cookies will be fully set in 3-4 hours as the butter solidifies.

STRAWBERRY CHEESECAKE COOKIES

1.5 cups salted butter room temperature
1 cup white sugar
1 cup light brown sugar
1 cup dark brown sugar
2 eggs
4 Tablespoons bakers brand imitation vanilla
4 cups all purpose flour
3 ounces instant vanilla pudding
3 Tablespoons cornstarch
2 Tablespoons Watkins Strawberry Extract
3 ounces chopped and grinded freeze dried strawberries
20 ounces cream cheese baking chips

Mix all of the wet ingredients with a mixer until well blended and fluffy and well combined, about 2 minutes. Add the dry ingredients to the wet. Blend ingredients by hand or mixer just until blended and all the white of the flower has been mixed in the wetness.

Now you want to refrigerate your dough in cling wrap/saran wrap for a minimum of 24 hours to a maximum of 72 hours. Do not skip this step. The ingredients get absorbed into each other and it makes for amazing science.

When you are ready to bake and allow your cookie dough to come to room temperature for about 1 hour. Preheat the oven to 415 and begin to scoop dough with an ice cream scoop sized to measure 2.0 ounces. Line your baking sheet with parchment paper and place 12 dough balls per sheet. This recipe will give you 35 sized 2 ounce scoops.

Bake for 11 minutes. Pull cookie sheet from the oven and allow cookies to come to a full cool at rest on the cookie sheet. Cookies will be fully set in 3-4 hours as the butter solidifies.

SUGAR COOKIE

2 sticks of salted butter
2 eggs
2 Tablespoons chosen flavor
1/2 cup white sugar
1/2 cup light brown sugar

Mix all of the wet ingredients until light and fluffy and very well combined.
Add to the same bowl:
4 cups all purpose flour
3 Tablespoons cornstarch

Blend dry ingredients into the wet until just mixed and all flour has been absorbed.
There is no need to refrigerate this dough.
Preheat the oven to 375.
Roll sugar cookie dough with an adjustable rolling pin to desired thickness. I use a .5 inch thickness and proceed to bake for 8 minutes on a parchment covered cookie sheet. As soon as cookies are removed from the oven, I flatten with a fondant smoother to help royal icing have a flat surface to adhere too.

ROYAL ICING

1/2 cup meringue powder
1 cup warm water
2 Tablespoons corn syrup
flavor of choice
8 cups powdered sugar

Add your powder sugar and meringue powder to the mixer and give it a few spins to mix them.

Add corn syrup and flavoring; continue to mix on low speed. While on low speed, slowly add 1/2 of the water. Once the first portion of the water is incorporated, slowly add the remainder. You may need to add another smidgen of water and that is okay.

Once all the water is added, move your mixer speed to 6-7 or med-high. Mix at that higher speed for about 3-5 minutes. The icing should reach a stiff peak consistency for very detailed designs. For florals you may need to add some more powdered sugar. For flooding consistency, you can remove some of the stiff peak consistency and then slowly with a spray bottle add small amounts of water at a time to get to 15 second icing. Color and bag icing.

ALMOND WEDDING CAKE

15 ounces Pillsbury Almond flavor cake mix
3 ounces instant vanilla pudding mix
4 eggs
2/3 cup vegetable oil
1 Tablespoon Watkins Almond extract
1 Tablespoon Lorann Almond flavor emulsion

The instructions for this cake are super easy. Basically, put all the ingredients into a bowl and mix it on medium speed for 2 minutes until combined and no lumps remain.

Pour batter into 9X13 or 2 9 inch round pans and bake at 350 for 40 minutes or until a toothpick inserted comes out clean.

Frost and decorate with your choice of buttercream or cream cheese.

COOKIE BUTTER CRUNCH CAKE

CAKE INGREDIENTS
15 ounces golden butter cake mix
3 ounces instant vanilla pudding
4 eggs
1 cup water
3/4 vegetable oil
2 Tablespoons Lorann Cookie Butter flavor emulsion

CAKE MIX IN INGREDIENTS
8 ounces broken Biscoff cookies

COOKIE BUTTER GANACHE
10 ounces Lotus Biscoff spread

COOKIE BUTTER CRUMBLE
8 ounces chopped Lotus biscoff cookies

BUTTERCREAM ADD IN
Add 1 Tablespoon Lorann Cookie Butter flavor emulsion to ingredients of cream cheese frosting or hybrid american buttercream.

Preheat the oven to 350 degrees. Mix all cake ingredients together in a mixing bowl. When well combined, add in the broken cookie pieces. Stir gently. You only want the cookie pieces blended in as while the cake bakes they will soften and be a nice surprise inside the cake.

Pour cake batter into a prepared 9x13 pan and proceed to bake for 40 minutes. Allow the cake to cool completely.

To make the ganache, heat the biscoff spread in the microwave for about 15 seconds and stir. When the spread has headed to a liquid state, pour all over the top of the cake.

Next is frosting. Either using my cream cheese frosting or hybrid american buttercream; add to those ingredients, the 1 tablespoon emulsion. Frost the cake as you like by spreading the icing or using a frosting bag with a piping tip.

Lastly, apply the crumbled biscoff cookies on top of the frosting or drizzle with any remaining cookie butter ganache.

CARROT CAKE

2 cups granulated sugar
1 cup vegetable oil
1 teaspoon pure vanilla extract
3 large eggs
2¾ cups all-purpose flour
2 tablespoons ground cinnamon
1 tablespoon ground nutmeg
2 teaspoons ground cloves
2 teaspoons baking soda
1 cup roughly chopped walnuts
2¼ cups finely grated carrots

Preheat the oven to 350°F. Grease and flour a 9x13-inch pan.

In the bowl of a stand mixer, beat together the sugar, oil, vanilla extract, and eggs until light yellow, about 3 minutes. In a separate bowl, sift together the flour, cinnamon, nutmeg, baking soda, and salt. With the mixer on low speed, slowly and gently add the dry ingredients to the wet mixture. Mix until just combined.

Remove the bowl from the mixer and fold in the walnuts and grated carrots.
Pour the batter into the prepared pan. Bake for 45 minutes. When cooled, frost and decorate with a choice of buttercream or cream cheese icing.

COFFEE CRUMB CAKE

CAKE INGREDIENTS
1/2 cup butter softened
3/4 cup sugar
1 tablespoon Lorann Butter Vanilla flavor emulsion
1 egg
2 cups flour
2 tsp baking powder
3/4 cup milk

INSIDE FILLING OF CAKE
3 tablespoons butter softened
3 tablespoons cinnamon
1/2 cup flour
1/2 cup packed brown sugar

CRUMB TOPPING
8 tablespoon butter softened
1.25 cup flour
2/3 cup packed brown sugar
1 cup chopped cinnamon baking chips
2 tablespoon cinnamon

Preheat the oven to 350 F. In the bowl of a mixer, cream together the butter and sugar, scraping down the sides occasionally. Add the vanilla and egg, mix in.

In a separate bowl, mix together the flour, baking powder and salt. Add one half of it to the mixer, and when mostly combined, add the milk. Once the milk is mostly incorporated, add the rest of the flour.

To make filling: in a small bowl, pinch together the softened butter, flour, sugar and cinnamon until soft crumbs form.

To make topping: add the butter, flour, brown sugar and cinnamon to a food processor and pulse until coarse crumbs form or cut in with a fork.

Grease a 9x9 baking pan. Pour in ½ of cake batter, and spread to all four corners. Sprinkle the filling over top, then pour in remaining cake batter. Sprinkle the topping over the top and press lightly so it adheres.

Bake in a preheated oven for 45 minutes. When out of the oven and cooled some, lightly dust with powdered sugar.

CREAM CHEESE FROSTING

16 ounces cream cheese room temperature
2 sticks butter at room temperature
2 teaspoons vanilla extract or flavor of choice
4 cups powdered sugar

In the bowl of a stand mixer fitted with the paddle attachment, beat the cream cheese and butter on medium-high speed until very light, creamy, and smooth. Scrape down the bottom and sides of the bowl to ensure no clumps remain. This process is about 5 minutes.

Add in the vanilla and beat until combined. On low speed, gradually add in the sugar and beat until fluffy, about 3 minutes. If the frosting is too thick, add a splash of milk or cream. If it's too thin, add more sifted powdered sugar.

HUMMINGBIRD CAKE

¾ cup unsalted butter, softened to room temperature
¾ cup vegetable oil
1 cup light brown sugar, firmly packed
½ cup white granulated sugar
2 large eggs
2 cups mashed overripe black/brown bananas (about 5 bananas)
1 (8 oz) can crushed pineapple (do not drain)
1 tablespoon vanilla extract
1 tablespoon LorAnn banana emulsion

3 cups all-purpose flour
1 teaspoon baking soda
1 teaspoon baking powder
2 tablespoons ground cinnamon
1½ cups chopped toasted pecans

In a mixing bowl, combine all the wet ingredients and mix until very well combined.

In a separate mixing bowl, whisk together all the dry ingredients.

Using a spatula, gradually fold the dry ingredients into the wet ingredients. Once about half of the flour mixture has been added, stir in the pecans. Mix until completely combined, but be careful not to over-mix, as this could result in a dry cake.

Bake at 350°F for 40 minutes in a 9x13 pan, or until a knife inserted into the center comes out clean.

Frost and decorate with a choice of buttercream or cream cheese frosting.

HYBRID AMERICAN BUTTERCREAM

32 ounces powdered sugar

2 cups of butter
1 ounce heavy whipping cream
3 tablespoons sweetened condensed milk
1 tablespoon corn syrup
1 tablespoon flavoring of your choice, if any

Whip the butter in your mixer until white light and fluffy, scraping the bowl down every minute for approximately 5 minutes.

Add in the remaining ingredients, cover your mixer with a towel, and mix for approx another 5 minutes scraping down the bowl as you go.

If you want a fluffier consistency you can continue to beat your buttercream for another 5-10 minutes.

ITALIAN CREAM CAKE

2⅔ cups all-purpose flour
2 cups granulated sugar
1 teaspoon baking powder
½ teaspoon baking soda
12 tablespoons unsalted butter, softened and cut into 12 pieces
1½ cups buttermilk
2 large eggs
1 teaspoon vanilla extract
2 tablespoons Watkins almond extract
1 cup sweetened shredded coconut

1 cup coarsely chopped pecans

Optional Cake Toppings:
½ cup pecan halves, finely chopped
½ cup toasted coconut, finely chopped

Preheat the oven to 350°F and thoroughly grease and flour a 9x13-inch pan.

In a large mixing bowl, combine the flour, sugar, baking powder, baking soda, and salt. Stir until completely combined. With the mixer on medium speed, add the butter one piece at a time, mixing until fully incorporated after each addition. The mixture will be sandy once all the butter is added.

Add the remaining ingredients to the mixing bowl. Scrape down the sides and mix until just combined; do not over-mix.

Pour the batter into the prepared baking pan and bake for 40 minutes, or until a toothpick comes out clean.

Frost or decorate with a choice of buttercream or cream cheese frosting.

ORANGE JUICE CAKE

3.5 ounce instant vanilla pudding mix
18 ounce yellow cake mix
4 eggs
2 Tablespoons Lorann Orange flavor emulsion
½ cup vegetable oil
1 cup cold water

GLAZE INGREDIENTS:
½ cup butter
¾ cup white sugar
¾ cup orange juice
2 Tablespoons Lorann Orange flavor emulsion

Preheat the oven to 350 degrees F. Grease a large bundt pan.

Combine all cake ingredients in a mixing bowl until well combined.
Pour batter into a bundt pan. Bake for 30 minutes, or until a knife inserted in the cake comes out clean.

Combine the glaze ingredients in a saucepan. Boil this mixture for about 2 minutes. While still warm, poke holes in the top of the cake with a fork. Pour orange juice mixture over cake.
When you are ready for cutting and serving, top with powdered sugar.

RED VELVET CAKE

15 ounces red velvet cake mix
3 ounces instant vanilla pudding mix
4 eggs
2/3 cup vegetable oil
2 Tablespoons Amoretti Red Velvet artisan flavor

The instructions for this cake are super easy. Basically, put all the ingredients into a bowl and mix it until combined and no lumps of pudding are left.

Pour batter into a 9X13 pan and bake at 350 for 40 minutes or until a toothpick inserted comes out clean.

Frost and decorate with a choice of buttercream or cream cheese icing.

RUM CAKE

2.5 cups chopped walnuts
15-ounce package yellow cake mix
3 ounces instant vanilla pudding mix
4 large eggs
1.5 cups dark rum - divided
¾ cup water - divided
½ cup vegetable oil

1 cup white sugar
½ cup light brown sugar
2 tablespoons LorAnn Rum Flavor emulsion
½ cup butter

Gather all ingredients and preheat the oven to 325°F. Grease and flour a 10-inch Bundt pan. Sprinkle the chopped walnuts and light brown sugar evenly over the bottom of the pan.

In a large bowl, combine the cake mix and pudding mix. Mix in the eggs, 1 cup of rum, ½ cup of water, LorAnn flavor emulsion, and vegetable oil until well blended. Pour the batter over the chopped nuts in the pan.

Bake in the preheated oven until a toothpick inserted into the cake comes out clean, about 1 hour.

To make the glaze, combine the sugar, butter, and remaining ¼ cup of water in a saucepan. Bring to a boil over medium heat; cook, stirring constantly, until it thickens and slightly darkens, about 5 minutes. Remove from heat and stir in the remaining ½ cup of rum.

Let the baked cake sit in the pan for 10 minutes, then invert it onto a serving plate.
Slowly pour the glaze over the cake until it reaches your desired level of soaking.

STRAWBERRY CRUNCH CAKE

CAKE INGREDIENTS
15 ounces strawberry cake mix
3 ounces instant vanilla pudding mix
2 Tablespoons Watkins Strawberry extract
4 eggs
1 cup water
3/4 cup oil
2.5 cups Dawn Strawberry filling (1 cup is for inside the cake mix, reserve the other 1.5 cups for a glaze when the cake is being frosted)

STRAWBERRY CRUNCH TOPPING
18 ounces golden oreo cookies, chopped into broken crumbled pieces
1 ounce freeze-dried strawberries
1 stick unsalted butter
6 ounces strawberry jello powder mix

Preheat your oven to 350 degrees and prepare your 9x13 baking pan.

In a large bowl, add all the cake ingredients and mix well. Pour into your prepared baking pan. Bake for 40 minutes or until a toothpick inserted near the center comes out clean.

While your cake bakes and cools, prepare the strawberry crunch topping. Add the cookies to a gallon freezer bag and break into chunky pieces. Add into the gallon bag your jello powder, pulverized freeze dried strawberries and the melted butter. Seal the freezer bag and mix all crunch toppings until well combined.

Once your cake is cooled, spread the remaining 1.5 cups Dawn strawberry filling over the top of the cake.

Then proceed to frost the cake with either the cream cheese frosting or hybrid american buttercream.

Sprinkle with the prepared strawberry crunch topping. The topping should completely cover the frosting.

BOURBON CHOCOLATE PECAN PIE

1 cup white sugar
1 cup light corn syrup
3/4 cup unsalted butter
4 large eggs
¼ cup bourbon
1 tablespoon Lorann Bourbon flavor oil
1 teaspoon vanilla extract
6 ounces semisweet chocolate chips

1 cup chopped pecans
1 cup whole pecans
1 unbaked 9" deep dish pie crust

Preheat the oven to 325 degrees.

For the pie filling, heat sugar, corn syrup, and butter in a small saucepan over medium heat, stirring constantly, until butter melts and sugar dissolves. Remove from the heat and cool slightly, about 5 minutes.

Whisk eggs, bourbon, flavor oil, vanilla together in a large bowl until well combined. Slowly pour sugar mixture into egg mixture, whisking constantly. Stir in chocolate chips and pecans.

Pour mixture into an unbaked pie shell. Top with whole pecans in a circle design.
Bake in the preheated oven until set and golden, 50 to 55 minutes. Serve warm or chilled.

BUTTERMILK CHESS PIE

2 cups white sugar
2 tablespoons all-purpose flour
5 eggs

⅔ cup buttermilk
½ cup melted butter
2 tablespoons LorAnn butter vanilla flavor emulsion
9 inch unbaked pie crust

Preheat the oven to 350°F.

In a large bowl, combine the sugar and flour. Beat in the eggs and buttermilk until blended. Stir in the melted butter and vanilla.

Pour the filling into the pie crust.

Bake in the preheated oven until the filling is set, about 45 minutes.

CHOCOLATE CHESS PIE

2 cups white sugar
2 tablespoons all-purpose flour
5 eggs
⅔ cup buttermilk
3/4 cup cocoa powder
½ cup melted butter
2 tablespoons LorAnn butter vanilla flavor emulsion
9 inch unbaked pie crust

Preheat the oven to 350°F.

In a large bowl, combine the sugar and flour. Beat in the eggs and buttermilk until blended. Stir in the melted butter, cocoa, and vanilla.

Pour the filling into the pie crust.

Bake in the preheated oven until the filling is set, about 45 minutes.

CHOCOLATE CREAM PIE

PIE CRUST INGREDIENTS
18 oz Teddy Graham chocolate graham crackers, crushed
5 tablespoons butter (melted)

CHOCOLATE PUDDING INGREDIENTS
⅓ cup granulated sugar
2½ cups whole milk
6 large egg yolks
2 tablespoons cornstarch
6 tablespoons butter
8 oz Merkens melting chocolate wafers
1 tablespoon vanilla extract

PIE CRUST INSTRUCTIONS

Preheat the oven to 350. Crush the graham crackers in a food processor until finely ground. Mix the crushed crackers with melted butter until well combined.

Press the mixture firmly into the bottom and up the sides of a 9-inch pie dish.
Bake for 10 minutes. Set aside to cool completely.

CHOCOLATE FILLING INSTRUCTIONS:

In a medium saucepan, combine sugar, milk, egg yolks, cornstarch, and butter.
Cook over medium-high heat (#7) while stirring constantly with a whisk to prevent sticking.

Once the mixture thickens to the consistency of mashed potatoes (about 5 minutes), remove from heat. Stir in the melting chocolate until fully melted and smooth. Add vanilla extract and mix well. Pour the pudding into the prepared pie crust.

Cover with plastic wrap to prevent a skin from forming on the pudding. Allow to cool at room temperature.

Top with stabilized whipped cream and serve.

COCONUT CREAM PIE

4 large egg yolks
2 cups whole milk
1/4 cup flour
2/3 cup granulated sugar
1 cup sweetened shredded coconut
2 Tablespoons butter softened
1 teaspoon pure vanilla extract
1 Tablespoon Lorann Coconut flavor emulsion
1 baked 9" deep dish pie crust

In a medium saucepan, combine all pudding ingredients. Cook over medium-high heat while stirring constantly with a whisk to prevent sticking. Once the mixture thickens to the consistency of mashed potatoes (about 5 minutes), remove from heat.

Pour the pudding into the prepared pie crust.

Cover with plastic wrap to prevent a skin from forming on the pudding.
Put the pie in the refrigerator for 4 hours overnight to cool completely and set.

Top with stabilized whipped cream and serve.

PUMPKIN PIE

15 ounces pumpkin puree
14 ounce sweetened condensed milk
2 large eggs
1 tablespoon ground cinnamon
½ teaspoon ground ginger
½ teaspoon ground nutmeg
1 tablespoon LorAnn pumpkin spice emulsion
1 unbaked 9" deep dish pie crust

Preheat the oven to 425 degrees F.

Whisk pumpkin puree, condensed milk, eggs, cinnamon, ginger, nutmeg, and emulsion together in a medium bowl until smooth.

Pour into the crust. Bake in the preheated oven for 15 minutes.

Reduce oven temperature to 350 degrees F and bake for 40 minutes. Let cool before serving.

Top with stabilized whipped cream.

SHORTBREAD PIE CRUST

1 cup butter
2 cups flour
¾ light brown sugar

Preheat the oven to 350.

Mix all ingredients until well combined.

Form a circle and transfer to a pie pan. Mold into crust.

Bake at 350 for 15 minutes.

STABILIZED WHIPPED CREAM

2 cups heavy whipping cream
½ cup powdered sugar
3 tablespoons instant pudding chosen flavor (white chocolate is my go-to)

Combine all ingredients into your mixing bowl. Mix on low for 30 seconds then speed up to high and continue to mix for approximately 4 minutes until stiff peaks form.

Spoon onto pie or transfer to a piping bag. Stabilized cream will hold its shape for days and will not become watery in the refrigerator.

BROWN BUTTER WHITE CHOCOLATE BLONDIE

12 tablespoons butter
1½ cups light brown sugar
2 eggs
2 tablespoons LorAnn butter flavor emulsion
1½ cups all-purpose flour
1 teaspoon baking powder
⅔ cup Merkens brand white chocolate, chopped

Preheat the oven to 350°F.

In a medium saucepan, melt the butter over medium heat. As it heats up, swirl the pan often. Once it starts to bubble, let it deepen in color for 3-4 minutes. You will see "browned spots" of butter; this is the process of making brown butter.

Remove the saucepan from heat and add the brown sugar. Stir for 1-2 minutes until the mixture is glossy and all of the brown sugar is dissolved into the butter.

Let the mixture cool. It can cool at room temperature or be placed in the refrigerator for 10-15 minutes. Ensure it reaches room temperature before adding the eggs to avoid scrambling them.

Add the eggs and LorAnn butter flavor emulsion; stir well.

Stir in the flour and baking powder. Mix well until combined.

Before adding the white chocolate, ensure the dough is chilled enough. You may want to refrigerate it for a few minutes.

Stir in the white chocolate and, if desired, optional pecans.

Line a 9x13-inch baking pan with foil or parchment paper. Bake until the top is shiny and slightly cracked, approximately 22 minutes.

COOKIES AND CREAM BROWNIES

OREO BROWNIE INGREDIENTS
3/4 cup unsalted butter
2 oz semi-sweet chocolate, coarsely chopped

2 cups sugar
3 large eggs room temperature
2 tsp vanilla extract
1 cup Hershey's Special Dark cocoa powder
1 cup all-purpose flour
15 oreo cookies chopped

COOKIE AND CREAM INGREDIENTS
12 oz white chocolate chips
6 tbsp heavy whipping cream
3 tablespoons powdered sugar
12 Oreos chopped

Preheat the oven to 350 degrees Fahrenheit. Grease a 9×13 inch pan or line it with parchment paper that sticks up above the sides, which can be used to lift the finished brownies out of the pan and make cutting easier. Set the pan aside.

Combine the butter and chocolate in a microwave safe bowl and heat in 20-30 second increments, stirring well after each, until melted and smooth.

Add the sugar and whisk until combined.

Add the eggs and vanilla extract and whisk together to combine.

Add the cocoa, flour and stir with a rubber or wooden spatula until well combined. Batter will be very thick. Stir in the chopped Oreos. Spread the batter evenly into the prepared pan, then bake for 28 minutes.

Set the brownies aside to cool. When mostly cool, make the cookies and cream layer.

Add the white chocolate chips and heavy whipping cream to a large microwave safe bowl and heat in 20-30 second increments, stirring well after each, until melted and smooth. Mixture will be thick. Stir in the powdered sugar and chopped Oreos, then spread evenly on top of the brownies. The mixture will be thick, just use your spatula to help spread it.

Allow the brownies to cool completely, then cut into squares. The cookies and cream layer will be quite firm to the touch, but great on top of the brownies.

FUDGE BROWNIE WITH BUTTERCREAM FROSTING

BROWNIE INGREDIENTS
1 ⅓ cups Dutch-processed cocoa powder
1 cup flour
1 teaspoon baking powder
1 teaspoon espresso powder
1 cup butter room temperature
2 cups white sugar
1 cup semi-sweet chocolate chips

2 Tablespoons Lorann Butter Vanilla emulsion
4 large eggs, room temperature

FROSTING INGREDIENTS
3 tablespoons butter room temperature
3 tablespoons cocoa powder
1 teaspoon vanilla extract
1 cup confectioners sugar
3 tablespoons heavy cream

Preheat the oven to 350°F and spray a 9x13-inch metal baking dish with nonstick cooking spray.
To a large bowl, add cocoa powder, flour, baking powder, and espresso powder. Whisk to combine. Set aside.

In a large saucepan over medium heat, add butter and sugar. Once the butter has melted, bring it to a low boil and cook for 2 more minutes, stirring occasionally or until it reaches 230°F on an instant-read thermometer. Remove from heat and stir in the chocolate chips and vanilla until completely melted. The mixture may still be grainy. Let cool for about 10 minutes.

Continue by adding eggs, one at a time, stirring constantly until smooth.
To the flour mixture, add the chocolate mixture. Mix until JUST combined.
Spread the batter into the baking dish and bake for 35 minutes until slightly puffed.

FROSTING INSTRUCTIONS

In a mixer combine room temperature butter, cocoa powder, honey, vanilla, and confectioners' sugar and mix on low speed for 30 seconds. Slowly add milk, one tablespoon at a time, until you reach the desired consistency. You may not need all 3 tablespoons, or you may need 1 more. It can vary from season to season and kitchen to kitchen.

Spread the frosting over the warm brownies.
Let the brownies cool completely before slicing and serving.

MISSISSIPPI MUD BROWNIE

1/3 cup unsweetened cocoa powder
1/2 cup vegetable oil
1/2 cup butter softened
2 cups granulated sugar
4 large eggs
2 tablespoons Lorann brand butter vanilla emulsion
1.5 cups all-purpose flour
1 teaspoon salt
3 cups mini marshmallows
1 cup chopped walnuts

For the Frosting:
1/2 cup butter melted
1/3 cup unsweetened cocoa powder

1/3 cup evaporated milk
1 teaspoon vanilla extract
3.5 cups powdered sugar

Preheat the oven to 350 degrees F. Grease a 9×13" pan with non-stick cooking spray.
In a large mixing bowl, pour oil over cocoa powder and mix.

Add softened butter and mix until smooth. Add sugar and mix for 1 minute. Add eggs, one at a time, mixing after each addition. Add vanilla and mix. Add flour and salt and stir to combine.

Pour batter into the prepared pan. Bake for 25-30 minutes or until a toothpick inserted into the center comes out clean.

Remove brownies from the oven and sprinkle the marshmallows evenly on top. Return to the oven for 2-3 minutes or until the marshmallows are puffed. Remove from the oven and allow them to cool completely.

Once brownies are cool, make the frosting.

Add melted butter, cocoa powder, evaporated milk, vanilla, and 2 cups of powdered sugar to a mixing bowl and beat with electric beaters until smooth. Add more powdered sugar, a cup at a time, mixing well, until you reach your desired frosting consistency. I usually use about 3 ¼ cups of powdered sugar.

Spread frosting over the cooled brownies and cut into squares. I've found a plastic knife works best to cut them. Also if you make them 1 day in advance they are much easier to cut.

PEANUT BUTTER BUCKEYE BROWNIES

BROWNIE BASE INGREDIENTS:
1 ⅓ cups Dutch-processed cocoa powder
1 cup flour
1 teaspoon baking powder
1 teaspoon espresso powder
1 cup butter room temperature
2 cups white sugar
1 cup semi-sweet chocolate chips
2 Tablespoons Lorann Butter Vanilla emulsion
4 large eggs, room temperature

BUCKEYE FILLING:
1/2 cup butter, softened
3/4 cup creamy peanut butter, (not natural peanut butter)
2 cups powdered sugar
2 teaspoons milk

CHOCOLATE GANACHE TOPPING:
1 cup semi-sweet chocolate chips
1/4 cup butter

Preheat the oven to 350°F and spray a 9x13-inch metal baking dish with nonstick cooking spray. To a large bowl, add cocoa powder, flour, baking powder, and espresso powder. Whisk to combine. Set aside.

In a large saucepan over medium heat, add butter and sugar. Once the butter has melted, bring it to a low boil and cook for 2 more minutes, stirring occasionally or until it reaches 230°F on an instant-read thermometer. Remove from heat and stir in the chocolate chips and vanilla until completely melted. The mixture may still be grainy. Let cool for about 10 minutes.

Continue by adding eggs, one at a time, stirring constantly until smooth. To the flour mixture, add the chocolate mixture. Mix until JUST combined. Spread the batter into the baking dish and bake for 35 minutes until slightly puffed. Allow to cool completely before the next step.

In a medium bowl, beat the filling ingredients with a hand mixer on medium speed until smooth. Spread mixture evenly over brownie layer. In a small microwave-safe bowl, microwave topping ingredients uncovered on High 30 to 60 seconds;

stir melted chocolate until smooth. Cool for 10 minutes; spread over peanut butter mixture.

Allow to set and cool completely 6 hours at room temp or 2 hours refrigerated.

SEVEN LAYER BARS

1.5 cups crushed graham cracker crumbs
1/2 cup butter
1 cup chocolate chips
1 cup butterscotch chips
1 cup sweetened flaked coconut
1/2 cup chopped walnuts
14 ounces sweetened condensed milk

Preheat the oven to 350 degrees. Spray a 9x13 inch baking pan with cooking spray or line with parchment paper and set aside.

Melt butter in a small saucepan. Remove from heat and stir in graham cracker crumbs until thoroughly combined. Press into the bottom of a 9x13 inch baking pan to form the crust.

Evenly sprinkle remaining ingredients one by one over the crust to form layers, beginning with the chocolate chips, followed by the butterscotch chips, coconut, and walnuts. Pour the condensed milk evenly over the top, and spread with a rubber spatula to make sure it's evenly distributed.

Bake in a preheated oven for 28 minutes until the edges are golden brown and the middle is set. Allow to cool completely before slicing.

CLASSIC PLAIN NO-BAKE CHEESECAKE

CHEESECAKE FILLING INGREDIENTS
24 ounces cream cheese softened to room temp
1.5 cups heavy whipping cream
1/2 cup granulated white sugar
3 Tablespoons powdered sugar
2 Tablespoons Loran vanilla bean paste

CRUST INGREDIENTS
18 ounces golden oreo well pulverized in food processor
1 stick of butter melted
1/4 white sugar

Stir together oreo crumbles and melted butter and mix well. Press into the bottom of a 9 inch springform pan. Spread up the walls of the pan and press into place. Chill until firm.

In your mixing bowl combine all cheesecake filling ingredients and mix until thick and creamy, to cheesecake consistency. Scrape down the sides of the bowl to incorporate well. Total mixing time is about 5 minutes.

Pour into a chilled crust and chill for 8 hours or overnight.

Just before serving, remove the sides of the springform pan.

Use stabilized whipped cream as a topping.

COOKIES & CREAM NO BAKE CHEESECAKE

CHEESECAKE FILLING INGREDIENTS
24 ounces cream cheese softened to room temp
2 cups heavy whipping cream
1/2 cup granulated white sugar
3 Tablespoons powdered sugar
2 Tablespoons Loran vanilla bean paste
18 ounces crushed oreos

CRUST INGREDIENTS
18 ounces chocolate oreo well pulverized in food processor
1 stick of butter melted
1/4 white sugar

Stir together oreo crumbles and melted butter and mix well. Press into the bottom of a 9 inch springform pan. Spread up the walls of the pan and press into place. Chill until firm.

In your mixing bowl combine all cheesecake filling ingredients and mix until thick and creamy, to cheesecake consistency. Scrape down the sides of the bowl to incorporate well. Total mixing time is about 5 minutes.

Pour into a chilled crust and chill for 8 hours or overnight.

Just before serving, remove the sides of the springform pan.

Use stabilized whipped cream as an optional topping.

DARK CHOCOLATE RASPBERRY NO-BAKE CHEESECAKE

CHEESECAKE FILLING INGREDIENTS
24 ounces cream cheese softened to room temp
2 cups heavy whipping cream
1/2 cup granulated white sugar
3 Tablespoons powdered sugar
2 Tablespoons imitation vanilla extract
1 cup dark cocoa powder

RASPBERRY GLAZE TOPPING INGREDIENTS
2 cups Dawn brand Raspberry flavor filling

CRUST INGREDIENTS
18 ounces chocolate teddy graham cookies pulverized in food processor
1 stick of butter melted
1/4 white sugar

Stir together cookie crumbles and melted butter and mix well. Press into the bottom of a 9 inch springform pan. Chill until firm.

In your stand mixer bowl combine all cheesecake filling ingredients and mix until thick and creamy, to cheesecake consistency. Scrape down the sides of the bowl until well incorporated. Total mixing time is about 5 minutes.

Pour into a chilled crust and top with 2 cups of raspberry filling. Chill for several hours or overnight.

Just before serving, remove the sides of the springform pan.

Use stabilized whipped cream for an optional topping.

LEMON NO BAKE CHEESECAKE

CHEESECAKE FILLING INGREDIENTS
24 ounces cream cheese softened to room temp
1.5 cups heavy whipping cream
1/2 cup granulated white sugar
3 Tablespoons powdered sugar
1 Tablespoon Watkins Lemon extract
2 cups Dawn brand Lemon filling (reserve 1/2 cup for on top of the cheesecake)

CRUST INGREDIENTS
18 ounces lemon oreo well pulverized in food processor
1 stick of butter melted
1/4 white sugar

Stir together oreo crumbles and melted butter and mix well. Press into the bottom of a 9 inch springform pan. Spread up the walls of the pan and press into place. Chill until firm.

In your mixing bowl combine all cheesecake filling ingredients and mix until thick and creamy, to cheesecake consistency. Scrape down the sides of the bowl to incorporate well. Total mixing time is about 5 minutes.

Pour into the chilled crust and top with remaining 1/2 cup lemon filling. Chill for 8 hours or overnight.

Just before serving, remove the sides of the springform pan.

Use stabilized whipped cream as an optional topping.

STRAWBERRY NO-BAKE CHEESECAKE

CHEESECAKE FILLING INGREDIENTS
24 ounces cream cheese softened to room temp
1.5 cups heavy whipping cream
1/2 cup granulated white sugar

3 Tablespoons powdered sugar
2 tablespoons watkins strawberry extract
2 cups Dawn brand strawberry filling (reserve 1/2 cup for topping the cheesecake)

CRUST INGREDIENTS
18 ounces golden oreo well pulverized in food processor
1 stick of butter melted
1/4 white sugar

Stir together oreo crumbles and melted butter and mix well. Press into the bottom of a 9 inch springform pan. Chill until firm.

In your stand mixer bowl combine all cheesecake filling ingredients and mix until thick and creamy, to cheesecake consistency.

Pour into the chilled crust and top with remaining 1/2 cup strawberry filling. Chill for several hours or overnight.

Just before serving, remove the sides of the springform pan.

Use stabilized whipped cream as an optional topper.

BANANA FLIP TWIN WHOOPIE

CAKE INGREDIENTS
15 ounce yellow cake mix cake mix
3 ounce instant banana pudding mix
2 Tablespoons Lorann Banana flavor emulsion
3 large eggs
¾ cup water
½ cup vegetable oil

FILLING INGREDIENTS
12 Tablespoons salted butter, room temperature
1¼ cup powdered sugar
1 dram Lorann Marshmallow flavor oil
2½ cups marshmallow fluff

Heat oven to 350°F. Line two large cookie sheets with either parchment paper.

In a large bowl, beat together cake mix, pudding mix, eggs, water and vegetable oil until thoroughly combined (batter will be thick).

Pour batter into a piping bag and proceed to pipe batter into 36 small circles onto cookie sheets about 1-inch apart (this will allow for spreading).

Bake 10 to 12 minutes until set. Cool completely before filling.

For the filling:
With an electric mixer on medium speed, beat butter and sugar together until fluffy then beat in marshmallow flavor. Beat in marshmallow fluff until incorporated. Refrigerate filling until slightly firm, about 30 minutes.

Once cookies are cooled, spread the filling on the flat side of one cookie. Top with the second cookie, flat side down to make a sandwich.

Wrap individually with cling wrap and store in the refrigerator.

BANANA PUDDING

14 oz sweetened condensed milk
1 ½ cups ice cold water
2 Tablespoons Lorann Banana flavor emulsion
3.4 ounces instant banana pudding mix
3 cups heavy whipping cream
4 cups sliced barely ripe bananas
12 ounces Nilla Wafer cookies

In a large bowl, beat together the sweetened condensed milk and water until well combined - about 1 minute. Add the pudding mix and beat well - about 2 minutes. Cover and refrigerate for 3-4 hours or overnight. It is very important to allow the proper amount of time for the pudding mixture to set. It will be watery if you don't let it set up long enough.

In a large bowl, whip the heavy cream until stiff peaks form. Gently fold the whipped cream into the pudding mixture until no streaks of pudding remain.

To assemble dessert in a 9x13 pan arrange 1/3 of the Nilla wafers covering the bottom. Next, layer 1/3 of the bananas, and 1/3 of the pudding mixture.

Repeat twice more, garnishing with additional wafers or wafer crumbs on the top layer. Cover tightly and allow to chill in the fridge for at least 4 hours - or up to 8 hours.

Banana slices will start to turn brown after 8 hours.

PEANUT BUTTER BUCKEYES

1.5 cups creamy peanut butter -- not natural peanut butter
6 Tablespoons butter softened to room temperature
1 teaspoon vanilla extract
3 cups powdered sugar

16 oz merkens brand dark chocolate

Line two half sheet pans with parchment paper or wax paper then set aside.

Add the peanut butter, softened butter, and vanilla extract to the bowl of an electric mixer, or to a large mixing bowl if using a handheld mixer, then beat on medium-high speed until creamy, 30 seconds. Add 2 cups powdered sugar, 1 cup at a time, beating on medium speed until combined between additions. Scrape down the sides of the bowl. Add the remaining 1 cup powdered sugar until the dough becomes very thick.

Scoop the dough out by the Tablespoon then roll into a ball and place onto the prepared sheet pans. If the dough becomes sticky, you can stick it in the freezer for 10 minutes. Once all the dough has been rolled into balls, place the sheet pans into the freezer to harden for 30 minutes.

Create a double boiler by adding a couple inches of water to a small saucepan then bringing it to a simmer. Place a heat-resistant bowl like a glass bowl or stainless steel mixing bowl on top, ensuring the bottom of the bowl doesn't touch the water, then add the chocolate to the bowl. Turn the heat down to low then stir the chocolate with a spatula until they're melted and smooth.

Working with one sheet pan of peanut butter balls at a time (leave the other one in the freezer), stick a toothpick in the center of a ball then dip it into the melted chocolate, leaving the top of the peanut butter ball exposed. Don't stick the toothpick in too far otherwise it will be hard to remove.

Gently spin the toothpick between your fingers to remove any excess chocolate then place the peanut butter ball back onto the baking sheet. Use your finger to gently press it off the toothpick. Repeat with remaining peanut butter balls then use your fingertip or a toothpick to smooth out the holes on top of the Buckeyes.

Refrigerate for 15-20 minutes to set the chocolate.

CANNOLI

CANNOLI SHELL INGREDIENTS
2 cups flour
1 ½ tablespoon granulated sugar
2 tablespoon butter
1 egg
½ cup white grape juice
1 tablespoon vinegar

CANNOLI CREAM FILLING
2 cups ricotta cheese drained

1 cup powdered sugar
½ teaspoon cinnamon

½ cup mini semi-sweet chocolate chips for garnish

Combine flour, sugar and salt in a mixing bowl. Add in butter and mix with a mixer until no large clumps remain. Mix in grape juice and egg. Transfer dough to a greased bowl and allow it to rest for 30 minutes.

Heat a large pot with vegetable oil. Oil should reach 355.

Roll dough out onto a floured surface. Dough should be very thin (about 1/16-inch). Use a 4 inch round cookie or biscuit cutter to cut dough out. Grease cannoli forms and wrap dough circles around each form. Brush half of the dough with an egg white and press dough around the form.

Carefully place each shell in the preheated oil. Fry until golden brown, about 1-2 minutes.

Remove shells from oil using metal tongs. Place on a paper towel. Use paper towels to remove the shells from the cannoli forms. Allow shells to cool before adding filling.

To make the filling, scoop the ricotta into a fine mesh strainer lined with a cheesecloth. Place the strainer over a bowl, cover the ricotta with the cheesecloth and then place a canned good on top to act as a press. Refrigerate for 12 hours to allow the liquid to drain.

Mix together ricotta, powdered sugar, cinnamon and vanilla. Scoop filling into a pastry bag. Pipe filling into the cannoli shells.

Dip filled cannoli into chocolate chips and sprinkle with powdered sugar.

CREAM HORN

15 ounce sheet frozen puff pastry, thawed
4 ounces cream cheese, softened
3 tablespoons white sugar
2 tablespoons Lorann vanilla bean paste
8 ounces marshmallow cream
1 tablespoon confectioners' sugar

Preheat the oven to 400 degrees F.

Unfold puff pastry sheet and use a pizza cutter to slice pastry into 6 even strips. Wrap each strip around a cream horn mold starting at the pointed end. Place rolled molds on a baking sheet with the end of the dough strip facing down.

Bake in the preheated oven until golden brown, about 12 minutes.

Remove horns from the oven and allow to cool to room temperature, about 20 minutes, before carefully removing molds.

Beat cream cheese, vanilla bean paste, and sugar together in a bowl using an electric mixer on medium speed for about 1 minute. Add in marshmallow cream and mix until blended.

Fill a pastry bag with cream filling and pipe filling evenly into each horn. Dust horns with confectioners' sugar. Refrigerate 30 minutes before serving.

TIRAMISU

COFFEE SOAK INGREDIENTS
2 cups strong brewed coffee still warm
½ cup coffee liqueur
2 Tablespoons Lorann Coffee flavor emulsion
2 tablespoons sugar

MASCARPONE FILLING INGREDIENTS
6 large egg yolks
1 cup granulated sugar
1 ½ cups heavy cream

2 cups mascarpone cheese, softened
1 tablespoon pure vanilla extract

ASSEMBLY INGREDIENTS
50 ladyfinger cookies savoiardi
Unsweetened cocoa powder
Dark chocolate shavings

To make the coffee soak, in a medium bowl, combine the brewed coffee, coffee liqueur, emulsion, and granulated sugar. Stir until the sugar is dissolved. Set aside to cool.

To make the filling, in a large heatproof bowl, whisk together the egg yolks and granulated sugar until well combined. Place the bowl over a pot of simmering water (double boiler method) and whisk continuously until the mixture is thickened and pale, about 5-7 minutes. Remove from heat and let it cool slightly.

In a separate bowl, whip the heavy cream until stiff peaks form. In another large bowl, beat the mascarpone cheese and vanilla extract until smooth. Gently fold the cooled egg yolk mixture into the mascarpone cheese until well combined. Fold in the whipped cream until the mixture is smooth and well combined.

To assemble, dip each ladyfinger into the coffee soak for about 2-3 seconds, ensuring they are fully soaked but not falling apart. Move quickly and use a fork under the ladyfinger to help lessen the breakage. Arrange a layer of soaked ladyfingers in the bottom of a 9x13-inch baking dish. Spread half of the mascarpone filling over the ladyfingers, smoothing it into an even layer. Repeat with another layer of soaked ladyfingers and the remaining mascarpone filling.

Cover and refrigerate the tiramisu for at least 4 hours, preferably overnight, to allow the flavors to meld together. Before serving, dust the top of the tiramisu generously with unsweetened cocoa powder and if desired, garnish with dark chocolate shavings.

Made in the USA
Columbia, SC
14 November 2024